This copy
of

How Will They Remember Me?

belongs to:

____

HOW WILL THEY REMEMBER ME?

Copyright © MCMXCIII

First Printing – April, 1993
Revised Edition – June, 1996

Printed in the United States of America.

Design and production by Ad Graphics • 800/368-6196

Library of Congress Catalog Number: 93-078044

ISBN 0-9636718-0-4

Published by Perry Publishing Co.
P. O. Box 52552
Tulsa, OK 74152-0552
(918) 747-9076 • (800) 329-9235
kimespeakr@aol.com

*A guide for experiencing a life
of meaning and purpose!*

Dedication

• • •

*In memory of Ben F. Bland, Wilbur Toone
and M.C. Cooke. They made a difference!*

Table of Contents

Testimonies

• • •

Steve Kime's book, *How Will They Remember Me?*, offers an excellent recipe for living each day of your life enthusiastically and optimistically. Steve has outlined a great "game plan of life" for those who refuse to accept a life of complacency and want to truly "make a difference."

C.L. Bowerman, Executive Vice President & CIO,
Phillips Petroleum Company

After dealing with the everyday pressures of life, reading Steve Kime's book *How Will They Remember Me?* offers the inspiration to make each new day the best it can be. It's a true winner in motivational material.

Steve Owens, 1969 Heisman Trophy Winner;
President, Steve Owens & Assoc.

In these days fraught with frustration and turmoil, it is refreshing to read the insights of an author who realizes one person can make a difference and has dedicated his life to doing just that. By telling about his experiences, Steve Kime is making a difference and is encouraging others to do the same.

Sharon J. Courtright, City Editor, Perry Daily Journal

How Will They Remember Me? is a thought-provoking book worthy of your undivided attention! Steve Kime presents guidelines for successful living. Inspiration abounds in the words of this book!

Larry James, Professional Speaker / Author,
LoveNotes for Lovers: Words That
Make Music for Two Hearts Dancing!

Acknowledgments

• • •

I am grateful for the opportunity to express in this book thoughts that have been in my heart for a long time. Writing a book has been a completely new experience for me, one I could never have managed without the help of many special people. I received guidance, strength and encouragement from these individuals. It's true! What goes around does eventually come around. As I have encouraged others, encouragement came back to me, enabling me to complete my first book project. Thank you all for "making a difference" in my life. I want to extend a special note of thanks to:

- Stephen Payne for sharing a book with me that "kick started" my engines. Thanks for helping me get on my "mission."

- Dave Patterson for sound writing advice, proofreading and encouragement. Rave On!

- Casey Lynn for letting me write during those times when you needed help with your homework.

- Cheryl Clinette for her research assistance and endless support. You're the greatest!

- Larry James for serving as mentor during this writing effort. Thanks for being accessible, Larry!

- Sylvester (the cat) for being great company during those nights and weekends spent writing.

- And the Father for his grace and mercy!

Forward

• • •

Every once in a while, something happens and life is never the same again. In some cases that is a positive experience and that is what Steve Kime's life is all about.

This book is Steve's contribution to making a difference in your life too.

Although Steve Kime and I met as a result of my response to a newspaper article, our association and friendship solidified rapidly because he really did make a difference. In my simple world, there are two kinds of people -givers and takers. Steve is a giver.

To that end, as he shares vignettes of life with us in this book, you know he has been there, done that, and is speaking from the heart. His recount of the Pikes Peak experience is thrilling simply because a nameless little lady cared to make a difference. You can now use that to trigger your "make a difference" efforts too. This book has pumped up my mind, turned on the motivation and helped me help others too. It has profoundly affected my behavior.

Because I know Steve personally, the book has extra meaning for me. He is your humble servant, doing what he preaches, making a difference. You can enjoy his book because it is real. This is where he lives.

You will like it.

I commend this book and Steve Kime to you for your personal enjoyment.

I promise, it will make a difference in your life too. Then, when you ask yourself "How Will They Remember Me?" you'll know you've made a difference.

This is a good thing.

Curtis L. Benton
Executive Vice President, Chief Operating Officer,
WESTELL Technologies, Chicago, Illinois

There is no meaning to life except the meaning man gives his life by the unfolding of his powers, by living productively.

... Erich Fromm

Introduction

• • •

As I have traveled across the country speaking to individuals from all walks of life, I have determined that even though we are uniquely different, there is one common denominator among us.

Deep inside us, there is a burning desire to experience a life of meaning and purpose. We want to know that our lives mattered and that our presence in this world made a difference. In the words of Oliver Wendell Holmes, "What lies behind us and what lies before us are tiny matters compared to what lies within us." I believe most people are hungry for recognition, comfort, security and perhaps wealth, but deep within us is that hunger to know that our community, churches, families and businesses are different because of our existence in this world. I truly believe we all want to be able to say, "I lived and my life mattered."

There are three reasons for writing this book. First, I want this book to be a source of strength for you when you get knocked down by the tough times of life. Tough times can show up at our front door at any time and just when we think all is well, WHAM, we get knocked down. Disappointment, adversity, the unfairness of life show up in our lives without an invitation. I want to help you get back up when you get knocked down!

Second, my hope is that this book will be a source of encouragement. My intent for the book is that it will serve as a driving force to challenge you to "keep on keeping on." If you are already experiencing a life that is making a difference, good for you! If you are successful in your career and community, great! If your life is on track, congratulations! Let me encourage you to "keep on keeping on. "

Finally, my hope is that this book will help you overcome a subtle but costly disease called complacency. Living a life of complacency, better known as "just going through the motions," can take the meaning and purpose out of an individual's life. I believe some individuals are wondering if there's a purpose to our existence beyond simply existing. The disease of complacency can lead to a life of boredom, futility and purposelessness. Perhaps this book will serve as a match that will ignite your pilot light, allowing you to light the burners to experience a life of meaning and purpose. This book is about giving your life meaning.

Benjamin Disraeli, the Prime Minister of Britian during the 1800s, once said, "The greatest good you can do for another is not just to share your riches but to reveal to him his own." Therefore, I hope this book will help you uncover the skills, abilities and resources you already possess, enabling you to make your contribution to this world. Begin to make a difference in this world, today! I am convinced you will find yourself enjoying life to the fullest and, more important, the people around you will find themselves influenced and affected by your presence in their midst.

On a personal note, congratulations on your vision, courage and determination. When you bought this book, you showed the will to succeed.

How
Will
They
Remember
Me?

> *If we are not to go to pieces or wither away, we all must have some purpose in life; for no man can live for himself alone.*
>
> ... Ross Parmenter

CHAPTER

ONE

FINDING A PURPOSE!

I believe there is more to life than just eating, sleeping and working. Our lives can be full of purpose and meaning. When our time on earth has ended, I believe we want to know that our time spent on earth was not wasted but was beneficial to mankind. The joy and peace in our hearts is almost indescribable when we realize that our lives made a difference.

Living a life that makes a difference can be defined differently by everyone. What making a difference means to me may not have the same significance or definition for you. I think it can be defined this way. Making a difference can simply mean living a life of meaning and purpose or achieving your full potential as an individual. Living a life of purpose allows each of us to believe that our presence in this world had an impact. It can mean experiencing a life of reaching your dreams and goals and participating in activities that enrich your life and the lives of others around you. Making a difference doesn't necessarily mean that you must find the cure for cancer or solve some environmental issue. Using your skills, talents and abilities in a way that enhances your life and the lives of those around you can make a difference. As John Gardner observed, "When people are serving, life is no longer meaningless."

Take a moment now and think of the individual who has had a significant impact on your life. Right now, as you are reading this book, pause and reflect upon that individual. Maybe you want to write that person's name down on a piece of paper. Think about the qualities that individual possess. Was he or she an example of integrity, honesty, or maybe just a source of encouragement to you? When I think of individuals who made a difference in my life, I think of my parents, teachers, coaches and neighbors. Each one affected my life in a unique way. But they all encouraged me to be the best I could be and helped me realize the importance of developing a character of quality. Time after time these individuals were accessible. I had the freedom to talk to them at any time. They were a source of help when I needed help.

There was a wealthy young boy who fell into a farm pond. The boy was thrashing around in the water and was about to drown. As he was pleading for help, a farm boy working in the vicinity of the pond pulled the other boy from the water, thus saving his life. The father wanted to meet the farm boy who was responsible for saving his son's life, and when they met, he asked the boy what he wanted to be when he grew up. The farm boy replied, "I want to be a doctor, but my family can't afford the cost of education so I will probably have to be a farmer." In gratitude for saving his son's life, the father paid all school expenses and the farm boy studied medicine and eventually became a doctor.

Years later, an important statesman traveling in the Middle East became seriously ill. The statesman had contracted pneumonia and needed the immediate attention of a qualified doctor. The doctor arrived and treated the seriously ill statesman. Before leaving his patient, the doctor took a long look at the face of his patient, recognizing him as the wealthy young boy he had saved from drowning many years ago. He had just saved his life for the second time.

Giving of yourself in order for others to achieve their dreams, helping others when in need, and using your skills and talents to assist others are just a few ways you can make a difference!

Let me ask you a thought-provoking question. Let's suppose that I'm in a room talking to a group of people comprised of your family members, neighbors and business associates. If I asked these people to name the individual who had a significant impact on their lives, would they mention your name? Please understand, I'm not suggesting that the only reason to be alive and do things for others is so they will mention your name. I want you to think about the contribution or impact your life may or may not be making on the lives of the people around you.

Individuals who have influenced my life include:

- ....

- ....

- ....

- ....

- ....

- ....

- ....

- ....

> *As a man
> thinketh so is
> he, and as a
> man chooseth
> so is he.*
>
> ... Emerson

C H A P T E R
Two

You are the Choices You Make!

The choices we make sometimes prevent us from making a positive difference in our own lives and the lives of others. You must realize that you are the choices you make. You are what you choose to be! You choose to be late, early, or positive or negative. You choose to set goals that enable you to reach your dreams, or you choose to just go through the motions, living a life of complacency. You can choose today to start looking within and identifying areas of your life in which you want to see some positive change. You can also choose just to leave things as they are. Earl Nightingale once said, "One of the most valuable things you can learn is that ultimately you're the one responsible for you." You are the choices you make.

I used to think that the only people who could make any difference were the intelligent, educated or lucky people. I also thought that only the good-looking people with the "right connections" could make a difference. I soon learned that the people who really made a difference in their own lives and other individuals' lives are the people who choose to!

Let me share this story with you regarding choices. Some time ago, a business associate of mine told me about an editor who might be interested in publishing one of my articles. My associate knew the type of speaking I did and suggested I submit an inspirational article to this editor, who had a preference for publishing positive, uplifting articles. When my friend suggested to me that I submit an article, I thought to myself, "There is no way in the world they would be interested in one of my articles." I remembered the times I had submitted other articles, only to be rejected. By this time I almost had myself convinced it would be a waste of time and effort.

One afternoon as I was sitting at my desk, I was thinking about a presentation I had given to some high school students. I remembered the emphasis I placed on the phrase, YOU ARE THE CHOICES YOU MAKE! I realized it was time for Steve to "practice what he preaches." I could choose to write the article and submit it or I could choose to do nothing. I chose to write!

Several months later I received a call from the editor, and much to my surprise, he wanted to publish my article. Not long after the article was printed, I received calls from North Dakota to New Jersey. The responses and comments from people were overwhelming. One letter I received said, "Thank you for making a difference in my life." After putting that letter away, I reflected upon the day several months ago when I made the decision to write and was so thankful that I chose to submit that article. Think of the loss for both the readers and me if I hadn't chosen to write!

Alfred Nobel, a Swedish chemist, was the inventor of dynamite. He made his fortune by inventing powerful explosives and licensing his formula to various governments for making weapons. One day, Alfred's brother passed away, and a local newspaper printed the obituary notice. The paper made a mistake. It printed the obituary of Alfred Nobel instead of his brother. The obituary listed all of the achievements of Nobel, like inventing dynamite and making his fortune by selling the formula to other countries, enabling them to design weapons. Nobel, on reading his own obituary, didn't like what he saw. He was distressed to think he would be remembered as an individual who was the creator of bombs, destruction and devastation. As a result, Alfred Nobel chose to change things and to make a difference. He took his fortune and established funding for the awards of Nobel Prize for Peace, Literature, and Medicine. These are what Nobel is known for today and not for his formulas for explosives. Alfred chose to make a difference in the way he would be remembered. Begin today to focus all of your energies and time on what you want to be remembered for.

Now, ask yourself this question: How will they remember me? It's a very tough question. Remember, the choices you make determine the answer to that question. Let me encourage you right now to choose to make a difference.

People association can prevent you and me from making a difference. I want to encourage you to associate with people with similar goals and dreams. Associate with successful and positive people. Join clubs or organizations with a group of people who have the same values. Fraternize with the kind of people who are on a "mission." These individuals will enhance and enrich your life. Make it a priority to spend time with people who will inspire you to "be your best" and who will stimulate mental growth. Let me suggest that you pick one or two people whom you admire and respect, then meet for lunch once a week. Incorporate weekly meetings with these individuals into your lifestyle.

A good example of surrounding yourself with people who will enhance and enrich your life took place in Barcelona, Spain, during the 1992 Summer Olympics. The event was the 400 meter race. Britain's Derek Redmond was running in this event when suddenly he fell down. With over a 100 meters to go, Derek looked up to see the other contestants running toward the finish line. Derek, experiencing a tremendous amount of pain because of a pulled hamstring muscle, was terribly disappointed over his inability to finish the race. Then a spectator came down out of the stands and helped Derek to his feet. Together, with the other man's support, Derek hobbled to the finish line. The man in the stands was Derek's father, Jim. Surround yourself with people who will enhance and enrich your life.

Choices I make today include:

- ....

- ....

- ....

- ....

- ....

- ....

- ....

- ....

*The tragedy of
life is what dies
inside a man
while he lives.*

... Albert Schweitzer

C H A P T E R

THREE

DEVELOP A WIT AND SAT ATTITUDE!

Getting started with making a difference in our lives usually begins with our attitudes. Many time we don't think we can change things. Because of low self-esteem or lack of confidence in ourselves, we tend to think "That's just the way things are and I can't do anything about it." This chapter is about believing in yourself. This could be one of the most important parts of the book for you.

In the words of Ralph Waldo Emerson, "Believe in yourself and what others think won't matter." It's important to understand that what you allow to influence your thinking affects your expectations, beliefs and attitudes. We need to see ourselves as winners! Vince Lombardi once said, "Unless a man believes in himself, makes a total commitment to his career and puts everything he has into it, he will never be successful at anything he undertakes." We must change our attitudes about ourselves and begin seeing ourselves accomplishing goals and enriching other peoples' lives.

When was the last time you stood in front of the mirror and said, "I like myself"? That long, huh! You need to get to a point in your life when you really like yourself! You need to have activities in your life that make you feel good and confident about who you are. Achieving goals is one way to help you build confidence in yourself and increase self-esteem. I will discuss later in the book the subject of goals.

I often suggest that individuals set aside 15 to 30 minutes to think about the significant achievements in their lives. I encourage you to take time to reflect upon the years in your life and write down on a piece of paper the events that you consider important achievements. It's very important for you to write what YOU think are notable accomplishments and not what other people have defined as accomplishments. A significant achievement may be the day the training wheels came off the bike, perhaps graduation from high school or college, or the times your children were born. The point is, list the personal achievements and read each achievement over and over to yourself. Read the list first thing in the morning and again in the evening before you go to bed. As you read these achievements to yourself, you are acknowledging these events as facts, therefore allowing your mind to store this positive information. When you remind yourself of past achievements, you begin to feel good about yourself. It works! It builds confidence! Set aside some time today to list your significant achievements and get ready to start feeling better about yourself!

Another way to increase your self-esteem and build

confidence in yourself is to incorporate the use of affirmation statements. Affirmations are very helpful in changing the message you give yourself. An affirmation is a powerful, positive statement that confirms a thought. The practice of acknowledging affirmations allows us to replace old, negative comments with new positive ideas and is a powerful way to change our attitudes! Affirmations can be spoken aloud, thought silently or even written down. Here are a few examples:

- Every day in every way I'm getting better and better.
- I love to love and be loved.
- Everything I need is already within me.
- I am vibrantly healthy.
- The more I give, the happier I feel.
- I like myself.
- I am a total winner.
- I am very creative in all areas of my life.
- I have an excellent memory.
- I am calm and confident in my interactions with others.

Affirmations can be instrumental in building confidence and self-esteem. This is one method I suggest you consider to help you achieve a positive attitude about yourself.

Another way to change the way you view yourself is to develop an SAT attitude. SAT is the acronym for SICK AND TIRED. Sick and tired of the way you look, the way you feel, the way your career is going, the condition of your finances. Develop an attitude that says, "I'm ready to change things."

I was visiting a friend the other day and she was sharing with me how "fed up" she had become with certain areas of her life. She complained about her situation and went on to say she had had enough! She was very unhappy with her life even to the point of being "fed up," but she wasn't changing anything. She was just complaining. There was no action on her part to change the situations. She hadn't reached the point of really being sick and tired. When you and I develop a SAT attitude, it should prompt us into action. By responding to that attitude, we begin to take steps to change things in our lives!

I believe you must develop this next essential attitude if you are going to reach your goals and make a difference in your life. It's called a WIT attitude. WIT means WHATEVER IT TAKES. This is a very popular phrase and it may be overused, but when you set goals in your life, you must be determined to reach them. I think you will see the importance of this attitude when we discuss GOALS later in the book. When the unfairness of life arrives at your home, when disappointment and adversity confront you, an attitude of "whatever it takes" will pull you through. It is practically impossible to slow down or stop anyone when he or she has a WIT attitude.

A great example of this attitude took place on February 6, 1982. A young women named Julie Moss was competing in the Ironman Triathlon event in Hawaii. This event consisted of a 2.4-mile swim, a 112-mile bike ride, and a 26.2-mile run. Sounds like a challenge to me! This event can take many grueling hours to complete. Julie Moss was 440 yards away from the finish line when she collapsed and fell down on the pavement. The finish line was in sight. Julie's body showed signs of dehydration and complete exhaustion. At this point Julie was in first place in the women's division. She took a moment to regain her composure and rose to her feet and proceded to the finish. Three hundred yards later she fell again. She was in such obvious pain that the spectators at the event and the television audience wondered how she could continue. Her muscles were cramped and her body was distorted from the day-long event. Her coach and the spectators had so much compassion for Julie that they wanted to help her finish the race. But if they helped her, she would be disqualified. Julie got up a second time and just staggered toward the finish, falling a third time just 50 feet from the finish tape. Then Julie Moss began to crawl on the pavement. Just before she crossed the line, another women, Kathleen McCartney, ran across and broke the winner's tape. Everyone watched Julie. Only a few noticed the other woman as she crossed the finish line first. All eyes were on Julie as she continued to crawl to the finish. Julie Moss had a WHATEVER IT TAKES attitude which enabled her to finish her race. With this type of determination and desire, you and I can truly make a difference in our lives and in this world.

As John D. Rockefeller expressed the idea, "I do not think there is any other quality so essential to success of any kind as the quality of perseverance."

My significant achievements include:

- ....

- ....

- ....

- ....

- ....

- ....

- ....

- ....

My personal affirmations are:

- ....

- ....

- ....

- ....

- ....

- ....

- ....

- ....

> *If one advances confidently in the direction of his dreams, and endeavors to live the life which he has imagined, he will meet with a success unexpected in common hours.*
>
> ... Henry David Thoreau

C H A P T E R

FOUR

GOALS HELP YOU REACH YOUR DREAMS!

Many times I call my personal and career goals my dreams! I have a vivid picture in my mind that is a dream, but eventually it evolves into a goal. An excitement enters our lives when we reach for our dreams.

I'm reminded of the words of Woodrow Wilson, "We grow by dreams. All big men are dreamers. They see things in the soft haze of a spring day, or in the red fire of a long winter's evening. Some of us let these great dreams die, but others nourish and protect them, nurse them through bad days till they bring them to the light which comes always to those who sincerely hope that their dreams will come true." Let me encourage you to turn your dreams into achievable goals today!

Goals give your life direction. Goals give you the drive and power to enable you to live a life of meaning and purpose. You must realize that you are responsible for the eventual outcome of your life. The goals and choices you have made in the past have brought you to your present circumstances. Remember this! Write it down! YOUR FUTURE IS DETERMINED BY THE GOALS YOU SET FOR YOURSELF TODAY! What you do or don't do today influences the events of tomorrow.

Striving to reach your goals gives your life meaning. I remember the time in my life when I spent more time planning my summer vacations and certain weekend outings than I did planning my future. Many people don't reach their goals because they don't consider their goals believable or achievable. I recommend that people write their goals down on paper and read them first thing every morning. Reading your goals to yourself will serve as a reminder of what you are working toward. It's worth saying again. YOUR FUTURE IS DETERMINED BY THE GOALS YOU SET FOR YOURSELF TODAY!

Once you have identified the area of your life that you want to improve, then set a goal. Decide what you want to become in that specific area of your life. Zig Ziglar once said, "What you get by reaching your goals isn't nearly as important as what you become by achieving them."

Several years ago I decided that my physique could stand some improvement. I decided to "commit to be fit." I incorporated some exercise into my lifestyle. The physique began to get smaller and 40 pounds later I felt much better. I didn't go on a strict diet or join a half dozen health clubs; I simply changed my diet and exercised daily. My goal to be fit made a difference in my life. I feel good physically which allows me to feel good mentally. I'm excited about the opportunities in life, and now I can meet those opportunities with a healthy body and attitude! Ben

Franklin once said, "To lengthen thy life, lessen thy meals."

I attended a high school football playoff game a few years ago, which I believe is a great example of what the pursuit of goals can do in our lives. This game would determine who would advance to the Championship finals. It was an action-packed game, certainly everything you would want to see in a playoff contest. With fewer than two minutes remaining in the game, the team behind on the scoreboard had the ball. They needed a touchdown to win! A field goal would not help. The offense had one specific goal: to travel 80 yards and score a touchdown. The defense had their goal: to stop the offense from scoring. After several tense and exciting plays, it appeared that the game winner would be determined on one final play. Thirty seconds remained on the game clock and it was fourth down. The offense needed about one foot to move the ball for a first down. Keep in mind that the offense and defense have their specific goals. The center snapped the ball, the quarterback pitched the ball to the running back and he started to run around the left end. Just before he crossed the line of scrimmage, he passed the ball to his teammate standing all alone in the end zone. Touchdown! The defense was focused on preventing a first down. The offense was determined to score a touchdown. I believe the defense and many fans in the stadium were focusing on the importance of stopping the offense from making a first down. They failed to see that the offense was determined to reach their goal, a touchdown. This type of determination displayed by a group of high school kids serves as a source of strength to me as I pursue my goals.

Set goals that are measurable and challenging but achievable. For example, set a goal to save $50 by the end of the month. Other examples include "I will give five hours of my time to volunteer service, I will make six new friends by the end of the year, I will read two books by the end of the month."

When you set goals, it's important to set a completion date or target date. You need to have the end in mind before you start. Set both short term and long term goals. Usually any goal under six months is considered a short term goal. Therefore, goals that will take six months and longer are known as long term goals. Completing college or paying off the mortgage are two examples of long term goals. The main emphasis here is to place a date on when you want to achieve your goal. When you have that date set, it will help motivate you to work hard and reach your specific goal.

When you begin your day by reading your goals, you will become focused on what task to accomplish. When you complete a goal, check it off! When you begin seeing the completion of goals and the check marks adding up, you will enhance your confidence and self-esteem. The accomplishment of reaching your goals will be evidence you are making a difference in your life.

I find the use of slogans and quotes to be sources of encouragement as I work toward my goals. Many years ago "Break 2 in 72" was a slogan that served as a powerful source of encouragement, strength and direction in my life. Everywhere I turned I saw the words "Break 2 in 72." I took small pieces of masking tape and wrote those four words across the tape. I placed the tape on the bedroom ceiling, by the kitchen sink, on the back door and on the dashboard of my car. Visualizing this slogan as I went through my daily routine kept me focused on my goals and gave me the mental strength to persevere.

Let me explain what "Break 2 in 72" actually means. As an athlete I had a goal to run 880 yards (a half-mile race) under 2 minutes and my date to complete this goal was in the year 1972. Thus "Break 2 in 72." As a student athlete, I recognized the significance of having numerous visual reminders displayed to help keep me focused as I worked on my educational and athletic goals. "Break 2 in 72" was a powerful slogan and the impact those four words had on me mentally shaped the next several years of my life. I can honestly say this slogan changed the direction of my life for the better. In case you are wondering, I did not "Break 2 in 72." I reached my goal in running the half-mile race under 2 minutes in May 1973. It took all of the work and discipline I developed in 1972 to reach my goal a year later.

Allow the words of a slogan or quote to become a part of you. Meditate, absorb and then apply the messages of these words to every facet of your life. They can be a source of strength as you work toward your goals! Henry Kaiser, the great industrialist, once said, "Decide what you want most of all out of life; then write down your goals and a plan to reach them." Don't you agree that right now is a good time to write down your goals?

My short term goals are:

- ....

- ....

- ....

- ....

- ....

- ....

- ....

- ....

My long term goals are:

—43—

- ....

- ....

- ....

- ....

- ....

- ....

- ....

- ....

> # *Only a life lived for others is the life worthwhile.*
>
> ... Albert Einstein

C H A P T E R

FIVE

How Can I "Make a Difference"?

There are several activities you and I can participate in that will make a difference in our lives and the lives of others. One of my favorite slogans is "Commit to Be Fit." If you want to make a difference in your own life, then become physically fit. When you feel good physically, you feel good mentally. You must take care of yourself physically, mentally and spiritually. Committing to be fit doesn't mean you must go out and join several health clubs. Just incorporate some physical activity into your lifestyle that will tone your muscles, relieve stress and condition your heart. Take a walk with a friend. Having a companion to exercise with will help you stay committed to your workout. You can encourage each other. However, before beginning any vigorous type of exercise program, it is wise to consult with your physician first. Remember, you have a lot to do and you need to be in shape to do it!

One way to make a difference in the lives of others is to write a book. Think for a moment of a book that changed your thinking, attitudes, or perhaps changed a facet of your life. I believe we all can name one book that has significantly affected our lives. Books have a powerful way of making a difference in our lives. Again, quoting Benjamin Franklin, "If you would not be forgotten as soon as you are dead, either write things worth reading, or do things worth writing." I think it's safe to say that books will stay around a long time. They will be here long after you and I are gone.

The same thing can be said about a song. Perhaps you need to write a song that will inspire, challenge or motivate other individuals. Words to music can really touch our hearts. When I hear songs like "The Battle Hymn of the Republic," "The Hallelujah Chorus" and even Buddy Holly's "True Love Ways," my heart is moved. Songs can speak to you in powerful ways, especially patriotic songs. Go ahead, write that song! Someone is wanting to be touched by your work. Life is a song that gives you a unique opportunity to contribute a verse. What will your verse be?

Another way to make a difference in your life and the life of others is to be a mentor. You have a wealth of information and experience you can share. Volunteer to teach a class that will enable you to share your expertise. When you do for others, you feel good about yourself. In the words of Kahil Gibran, "You give but little when you give of your possessions. It is when you give of yourself that you truly give." Be available; there are plenty of opportunities in your community to offer your talents to share with and instruct others. Don't wait any longer! It was Andrew Carnegie who said, "No man can become rich without himself enriching others." Share your vast knowledge with others today!

This may sound a little strange, but planting trees can make a difference in this world. Besides helping the environment, you will be helping other creatures too! Over 25 years ago I participated in a school project planting pecan trees. I took home ten pecan seedlings and planted them in different areas of our very large yard. Only one tree survived, but it stands straight and tall today. It's a huge tree that provides shade in the summer and pecans for the squirrels (since they are usually first to get them) and for neighbors in the late fall. People and animals are enjoying my tree planting efforts from more than 25 years ago. Planting trees can be fun with family or friends. Find an area where trees need to be planted and make it a ceremonial day by planting trees. Years from now you will be glad you took time to give a seedling a chance to become a towering tree!

I am reminded of a story about a young traveler exploring the French Alps. During his journey, the young traveler came upon a stretch of land that was flat and desolate. The land was extremely barren and offered nothing to explore for the traveler. As the traveler was turning back to go home, he noticed an old man out in this desolate land with a sack of acorns. It appeared the old man was planting these acorns in the ground. He would walk a few steps, stop and plant another acorn. The young traveler became very curious about what the old man was doing, so he decided to go have a talk with him. The traveler learned that the old man had planted 100,000 acorns. The old man said he wanted to spend the final years of his life doing something beneficial to mankind.

Many years later, the traveler had the opportunity to return to this desolate area. He couldn't believe his eyes as he was retracing his steps from his previous journey. The land that was barren now contained a wooded forest that was ten square miles. The traveler stood in amazement looking at the results of that old man who just wanted to do something useful for others to enjoy.

Perhaps you have an invention or personal discovery you could share with the world. Think of the inventions, devices and the technical achievements that have benefitted mankind. The telephone, toothbrush and typewriter all started with an idea. What is your idea? What invention do you want to bring into existence? Let me encourage you to follow through with your ideas. You never know, maybe your invention or idea could change the lives of many.

Speaking a word of encouragement is one significant way to make a difference in other peoples' lives. The power of the spoken word is incredible. I really don't think we can say enough good things to our family members, co-workers and neighbors. Words of encouragement, kindness and thoughtfulness can do so much in building relationships. The statements, "you're looking good today, you did a super job, thank you for your hard work," can mean so much to a person who hears negative comments all the time. You know how much you enjoy receiving a compliment. Make a difference in someone's life today by simply speaking a word of encouragement. I believe Olympic Gold medalist swimmer Janet Evans summed it up when she said, "Winning gold medals is great, but knowing that something you said might have positively changed someone's life was an even greater feeling." Go ahead, make someone's day!

The only prerequisite for making these activities work in your life is your commitment to get up and take action! There is a story about a woman who was stranded at the Paris airport. The woman was very distraught, depressed and was sitting in a chair at the airport crying. A young couple came along and began to ask her what was wrong. The woman told the young couple she had lost her plane ticket and she didn't know how she would be able to get home. Since the woman had spent all of her money, she was unable to buy something to eat for that day. So the couple invited her to join them for a sandwich and coffee at the airport restaurant. While at the restaurant they could discuss what could be done to help the lady get home. As the three of them got up and started toward the restaurant, the woman who had lost her ticket began screaming hysterically. She said, "Look, there's my ticket. I've been sitting on it all this time."

You and I will need to get up off our "tickets" if we are going to make a difference. You must take action!

I can "make a difference" by participating in these activities:

- ....

- ....

- ....

- ....

- ....

- ....

- ....

- ....

> *The greatest accomplishment is not in never falling, but in rising after you fall.*
>
> ... Vince Lombardi

CHAPTER

SIX

OVERCOMING ADVERSITY!

All of us face obstacles at times that seem insurmountable. Adversity, the unfairness of life, mistakes and disappointments can come as obstacles that can knock us off our feet. These obstacles can be a source of strength or they can bring defeat into our lives. In the words of Theodore Roosevelt, "The only man who never makes a mistake is the man who never does anything." Successful people make as many mistakes as "not so" successful people. The only difference is successful people acknowledge their mistakes, laugh at them and then learn from the mistakes. Remember, adversity can teach us a great deal about ourselves. It's possible to learn more from our failures and defeats than our successes. Life can makes us bitter or better.

Right now, you may be in a very difficult situation. You may be experiencing all of life's unfairness and disappointments. You may be wondering how you will ever resolve this problem. You could be thinking, "Life is really tough and I don't know how I will ever overcome this obstacle." Let me say to you, KEEP ON KEEPING ON! In the book *Twice Pardoned*, Harold Morris tells of his experiences dealing with adversity. Morris was sentenced to prison to face two life terms. The book gives a personal account of how Harold Morris, an inmate in the Georgia State Penitentiary, survived the best and worst years of his life imprisoned for murders he did not commit. I recommend you take the time to read this book. It will encourage you as you face adversity.

A farmer planted a section of land with wheat each year. There was a large rock in one of his fields, forcing the farmer to plant around it. In preparing the field, the farmer had damaged several plows as he accidentally hit the rock. After breaking another plowshare, the farmer decided to do something about this rock. It was time to remove this obstacle. The farmer placed a pry bar underneath the rock and, to his amazement, found the rock to be only a few inches thick. He was able to break it up with a hammer. The farmer realized he could have removed this obstacle if he had confronted it earlier.

Let me encourage you to face this day and all of its obstacles head on! Don't delay confronting the obstacle that may be in your life! The disappointments will soon fade and moments of joy will replace them. The overwhelming problems will eventually be disguised as "lessons in life." As we live our lives, we will continually be learning lessons. That wealth of insight we gain from these lessons will be the wisdom to share with our families and friends. Let me share with you some wisdom that I received from my "lessons in life."

As an encourager, let me offer a few suggestions to help you get on track and feel good about yourself. Personally, I remember a time when I really wanted a second chance in life. I wanted a second chance specifically in rebuilding relationships. I was looking for someone to give me another chance, but I couldn't find anyone willing. Later I realized that I was actually the person who should give me another chance. For some reason I kept thinking that I needed someone else to give me the okay to start again. I decided in my mind that Steve Kime would go ahead and give himself another opportunity. Don't wait for permission from someone else when you're ready to get on track. Today, forgive yourself for your mistakes and defeats. No matter what they were and no matter how difficult this task may be, FORGIVE YOUR-SELF right now! You deserve a second chance! Give yourself another opportunity to make a new start. Whether it's in relationships with others or with yourself, start today to build the type of relationships you desire.

Remember, you can't change what happened five minutes ago. You can't change what took place five months or five years ago, but you can start right now to make today and the rest of your life what you want it to be!

One effective method to stay on track and to motivate yourself is to read inspirational and self-help material. Take control of what goes into your mind. I remember a time in my life when my reading diet consisted of the sports page from the local newspaper. On certain days I would expand my horizons by browsing the classified section. I stayed in tune with the sports world, but I didn't have any awareness of what was happening out in the real world. I recall seeing a comic in a computer publication which contained a humorous picture with this caption: "Garbage In, Garbage Out." It may be time for you to watch less television and fill that time by reading inspirational books. *There's A Better Way to Live* by Og Mandino and *The Magic of Thinking Big* by David J. Schwartz, Ph.D. are two books I recommend. According to James McCosh, "The book to read is not the one which thinks for you, but the one which makes you think!" Replace the "negative" that goes into your mind by reading positive, motivating and personal growth material. I encourage you to spend at least one hour a day reading material that will inspire you and help you to grow. In the words of Stephen Covey, "The person who doesn't read is no better off than the person who can't read."

When taking that next long distance trip in your car, take along some audio cassettes. Listen to tapes that contain stories from motivational speakers. I enjoy listening to the "Oldies station" as much as the next person, but tapes with messages on affirmation, self-help and goal setting can really encourage you. Thirty minutes spent listening to an inspiring story can really help you through the day. Remember, listening to a tape is the next best thing to being there. You can feel a sense of one-on-one communication with the speaker since you are the sole audience.

When you have the opportunity to attend a seminar or class, do it! Seminars can offer a great deal of encouragement. The subject matter is always positive and uplifting. You have the opportunity to associate with motivated and successful people. You can learn and grow from attending various classes and seminars. One of the costly errors we can make is to assume our learning capacity is over after completing our formal education. I think it's essential to attend classes or seminars if you are determined to make a difference in your life and in the lives of others. Learn all you can, in all the ways you can, in all the places you can, as long as you can.

Books I want to read include:

- ....

- ....

- ....

- ....

- ....

- ....

- ....

- ....

Seminars I want to attend include:

• ....

• ....

• ....

• ....

• ....

• ....

• ....

• ....

> *But they that wait upon the Lord shall renew their strength; they shall mount up with wings as eagles; they shall run, and not be weary; and they shall walk, and not faint.*
>
> ... Isaiah 40:31   (Scripture quote from the King James Version of the Bible)

CHAPTER
SEVEN

RUNNING UP PIKES PEAK!

I would like to share my experience with you regarding running up to the Summit of Pikes Peak and my encounter with a "difference maker." After 4 hours and 26 minutes of running up the side of a mountain and covering a distance of 13.4 miles of rocky terrain, I crossed the finish line at the annual Pikes Peak Ascent Run held in the Colorado Rockies. As I staggered under the finish line banner at an altitude of 14,110 feet, a race official placed the "finishers" medal around my neck and said, "Now, feel good about yourself, Steve!" Even though I was extremely exhausted (physically and mentally), I regained my senses (and consciousness) and did exactly what the race official suggested. I did feel good about myself! I had just completed reaching a personal goal and put my name in the record books as a "survivor" in running up Pikes Peak!

Minutes after reaching the summit of Pikes Peak I took a few minutes to reflect on my accomplishment. I also took a few minutes to obtain some medical assistance and locate a tank of oxygen so I could adjust to the thin air complications my body was experiencing. Even though I ran, crawled, and staggered every step up the mountain by myself, I recall those dear words of a runner that encouraged me when I was ready to quit. Those words of encouragement by this "difference maker" will always be etched on my mind. I think you'll agree, words of encouragement can go a long way!

About four hours into the race and approximately two miles from the finish line my body decided it couldn't go any farther. I was completely exhausted. Every bit of my physical, mental and emotional being was depleted. I had trained extensively for seven months in preparation for running the race. At around 12, 000 feet my body had convinced my mind "You can't go on Steve." Words cannot describe the level of exhaustion my body was experiencing. I had trained and prepared for this event, but I had reached my limit.

Picture this in your mind. Think of a grown man on a path on the side of a rocky mountain: he is leaning against a boulder ready to break down in tears. That man is me. I am so tired I cannot go on with the race. Looking up at the distant summit, I know there is no way I can reach the top. Wanting to cry, I sit down in disbelief that I had gotten myself into this predicament. Already I had run 10 miles up the mountain so I can't go down, and I don't have the strength to go up to reach the summit. How did I get myself in this situation? I keep thinking, "I wonder if I could afford to pay a helicopter service to get me down off this mountain?"

As I'm leaning across the boulder having a pity party, I hear the sounds of feet shuffling or running on the rocky path next to me. Another runner is about to pass me. Just as the runner passes by she says, "Come on, Okie, you can do it. Just two miles to go!" When she went by, I gathered enough strength to ask her a few questions. I learned she was a 67 year old grandmother from the state of Arkansas – humbling to a 39 year old man to see Grandma pass you during the race. By the way, this was her seventh time to race up Pikes Peak. She shares this bit of news with me as I still lie clinging on to the boulder. Her radiant smile and words of encouragement simply "kick start my engines." Those timely words of inspiration "Come on, Okie, you can do it" served as the "push" I needed to get up and finish the race. This difference maker, the 67 year old woman, went on up the mountain and I followed later in her steps.

I can't explain why those words had such an impact, but they made all the difference to me. Those words came at a time when nothing else would do. In my opinion, that grandmother was truly a "difference maker." I am taking to heart the lesson I learned at 12,000 feet, the lesson to be a source of encouragement to everyone I meet, no matter what the elevation. When you find yourself in a predicament, when you're ready to quit and when you think you can't go on any further, just remember I'm cheering for you. Can you hear me saying, "Come on, you can do it?"

I started this chapter with a reference to a scripture taken from the book of Isaiah in the Bible. Encouragement came to me in two ways enabling me to finish the race: the grandmother and her words of inspiration I mentioned earlier in this chapter and the words of this verse found in the Old Testament.

Approximately 50 yards from the finish line was a small cardboard sign with the words, "But they that wait upon the Lord." About 10 yards later was another sign with the words "shall renew their strength." As I approached the finish, I noticed the remaining signs with the remaining words to this Bible verse. It's difficult to express the inspiration I received by reading those words as I was nearing the Summit.

I made it to the mountain top of Pikes Peak! With the encouraging words of a grandmother and the words from an Old Testament prophet, I was able to acheive this goal. No matter how dark and difficult the situation is that you may be experiencing, be mindful there lies a source of strength and encouragement nearby. Let me encourage you to take a moment and look for the signs!

EPILOGUE

As I stated in the introduction to the book, I want to help you uncover the talents and skills you already possess, enabling you to experience a life of meaning and purpose. I hope I have succeeded in this task. I sincerely believe that if you follow the guidelines in this book, you will begin to experience positive changes in your life. Take it a step at a time. Begin by taking a few moments to think of the contribution or impact you want to make on the lives of the people around you. Reflect upon the individuals who have influenced your life. Think of the qualities you admire in that person.

Next, choose to "make a difference" in your life. YOU ARE THE CHOICES YOU MAKE! Associate with the kind of people who will inspire you to "be your best." Make it a priority to associate with people who have similar goals and dreams.

Believe in yourself! You are special! If you look around, you will notice that no one smiles like you, combs his or her hair like you do or even dresses like you. You are unique! There is value in rarity! Therefore, you are valuable! It's time you stood in front of the mirror and said, "You've got the right stuff, baby!"

Incorporate affirmation statements in your life. This will build your self-confidence and self-esteem. Develop a SAT attitude that says, "I'm SICK AND TIRED of the way things are going, and I'm going to change things in my life." Do WHATEVER IT TAKES to reach your dreams. Develop a WIT attitude to "make a difference" in your life and the lives of others. Goals will give your life direction. Therefore, set specific, challenging and achievable goals in your personal and professional life today!

Experience a life of meaning and purpose by participating in activities of your choice. "Commit to be fit," write a book, share your song, volunteer or share your invention with the world. Get off your "ticket" and experience a life of purpose.

Be prepared for obstacles but face them head on! Read inspirational books, listen to motivational tapes and attend personal growth seminars. These activities will strengthen you as you face difficulties and adversities.

When encountering new information, you must apply what you have learned in your life. Now you must act. You can read the greatest book ever written, you may be a student of the world's most famous professor, but until you take that information and apply it to your life, no growth or change will take place. It is now time to take action!

There was a very talented musician who could play the world's finest violin, a Stradivarius. This musician had a unique gift for bringing out the finest from this violin. In the hands of this musician, the violin touched the hearts of all who heard it.

One day the musician donated this extraordinary violin to the city for all citizens to view and admire. Upon donating the violin, the musician requested that the violin remain stored in its beautiful case, never to be played again. The violin no longer was used as an instrument to bring pleasurable music to the ears of the listener. Its purpose now was to be placed on display for all the citizens to see. All that remains of the violin today are dust particles. Inside the beautiful case is wood dust that used to be the Stradivarius. Wood that is disregarded and never used eventually turns to dust. And so it is with the things we have learned. If you don't apply what you've learned, it to will eventually disintegrate. Take action today!

You can realize a life of meaning and purpose. Let me encourage you to experience a life that "makes a difference." You are somebody! This world needs you! This world needs your talents, your ideas, wisdom and most of all, your contributions to mankind that only you can give. You are somebody who can "make a difference"!

You live only when you have a purpose. According to Oswald Spengler, "This is our purpose: to make as meaningful as possible this life that has been bestowed upon us; to live in such a way we may be proud of ourselves; to act in such a way that some part of us lives on." I wish you the best as you experience your life of meaning and purpose. How will they remember me? Perhaps, now is a good time to think of your answer.

I shall close with a quote that I used when signing off the air as a radio personality. It is a quote that inspired me to "make a difference." In the words of Ralph Waldo Emerson, "To have a friend is to be one."

The End

QUOTES OF ENCOURAGEMENT

QUOTES OF ENCOURAGEMENT

AIM

First say to yourself what you would be; and then do what you have to do. — *Epictetus*

AMBITION

Keep away from people who try to belittle your ambitions. Small people always do that, but the really great make you feel that you, too, can become great. — *Mark Twain*

BROTHERHOOD

To live is not to live for oneself alone; let us help one another. — *Menander*

CHARITY

You must give some time to your fellow men. Even if it's a little thing, do something for others—something for which you get no pay but the privilege of doing it. — *Albert Schweitzer*

COMMUNICATION

If you have a friend worth loving, Love him. Yes, and let him know That you love him, ere life's evening Tinge his brow with sunset glow. Why should good words ne'er be said Of a friend till he is dead? — Daniel W. Hoyt

COMPLIMENT ONE ANOTHER

Learn how to pay compliments. Start with the members of your family, and you will find it will become easier later in life to compliment others. It's a great asset.
— Letitia Baldrige

CONSIDERATION FOR OTHERS

Always be nice to people on the way up because you'll meet the same people on the way down.
— Wilson Mizner

If you cannot lift the load off another's back, do not walk away. Try to lighten it. — Frank Tyger

DEDICATION

Whatever your career may be, do not let yourself become tainted by a deprecating and barren skepticism, do not let yourself be discouraged by the sadness of certain hours which pass over nations. . . .Say to yourself first, "What have I done for my instruction?" and as you gradually advance, "What have I done for my country?" until the time comes when you may have the immense happiness of thinking that you have contributed in some way to the

progress and to the good of humanity. But whether our efforts are, or not, favored by life, let us be able to say, when we come near to the great goal, "I have done what I could."
— Louis Pasteur

DESPAIR

When you get into a tight place and everything goes against you, till it seems you could not hold on a minute longer, never give up then, for that is just the place and time that the tide will turn.   — Harriet Beecher Stowe

DREAMS

If you have built castles in the air, your work need not be lost; that is where they should be. Now put the foundations under them.   — Henry David Thoreau

GOALS GIVE OUR LIVES DIRECTION

We need focus and direction. Most of all, we need the sense of accomplishment that comes from achieving what we set out to do ... it's important to make plans, even if we decide to change them, so that at least for the moment we know where we're going and we can have a sense of progress.
— Leon Tec, M.D.

THE GOLDEN RULE

All things whatsoever ye would that men should do to you, do ye even so to them: for this is the Law and the Prophets.
— Jesus of Nazareth

KINDNESS

Do not wait for extraordinary circumstances to do good; try to use ordinary situations.   *— Jean Paul Richter*

LIFE

You can't do anything about the length of your life, but you can do something about it's width and depth.

— Evan Esar

MISTAKES ARE A PART OF LIFE!

When you make a mistake, don't look back at it long. Take the reason of the thing into your mind, and then look forward. Mistakes are lessons of wisdom. The past cannot be changed. The future is yet in your power.

— Hugh White

If you have made mistakes, even serious mistakes, there is always another chance for you. And supposing you have tried and failed again and again, you may have a fresh start any moment you choose, for this thing that we call "failure" is not the falling down, but the staying down.

— Mary Pickford

SAY GOOD-BYE TO THE PAST!

Finish each day and be done with it. You have done what you could. Some blunders and absurdities no doubt crept in; forget them as soon as you can. Tomorrow is a new day; begin it well and serenely and with too high a spirit to be cumbered with your old nonsense.

— Ralph Waldo Emerson

PERSEVERANCE

Nothing in the world can take the place of perseverance. Talent will not; nothing is more common than unsuccessful men with talent. Genius will not; unrewarded genius is almost a proverb. Persistence and determination alone are omnipotent. — Calvin Coolidge

If a first you don't succeed,
Try, try again;
Then your courage should appear,
For, if you will persevere,
You will conquer, never fear;
Try, try again. — W.E. Hickson

Don't be discouraged by a failure. It can be a positive experience. Failure is, in a sense, the highway to success, inasmuch as every discovery of what is false leads us to seek earnestly after what is true, and every fresh experience points out some form of error which we shall afterwards carefully avoid. — John Keats

REGRETS

You cannot go around and keep score. If you keep score on the good things and the bad things, you'll find out that you're a very miserable person. God gave man the ability to forget, which is one of the greatest attributes you have. Because if you remember everything that's happened to you, you generally remember that which is the most unfortunate. — Hubert H. Humphrey

SELF-ESTEEM

If you want to be respected, you must respect yourself.
—Spanish proverb

Use what talents you possess: the woods would be very silent if no birds sang there except those that sang best.
– Henry Van Dyke

SERVICE TO ONE ANOTHER

One thing I know: the only ones among you who will be really happy are those who will have sought and found how to serve.
– Albert Schweitzer

Dedicate some of your life to others. Your dedication will not be a sacrifice. It will be an exhilarating experience because it is an intense effort applied toward a meaningful end.
– Dr. Thomas Dooley

SUCCESS IS CONTAGIOUS!

Success is a trendy word. Don't aim for success if you want it; just do what you love and it will come naturally.
– David Frost

Whatever you are by nature, keep to it; never desert your line of talent. Be what nature intended you for and you will succeed.
– Sydney Smith

TALENTS SHOULD BE USED!

Hide not your talents, they for use were made. What's a Sun-dial in the shade?
– Benjamin Franklin

If you have a talent, use it in every which way possible. Don't hoard it. Don't dole it out like a miser. Spend it lavishly like a millionaire intent on going broke.
– Brendan Francis

TIME

Time is the coin of your life. It is the only coin you have, and only you can determine how it will be spent. Be careful lest you let other people spend it for you.
– Carl Sandburg

PRODUCTS AVAILABLE FROM STEVE KIME INCLUDE:

HOW WILL THEY REMEMBER ME?

A guide for experiencing a life of meaning and purpose!

This book contains stories of inspiration and encouragement. It will help you handle the disappointments and adversities in life. This book will challenge you to overcome a life of complacency and experience a life of meaning and purpose.

BREAK 2 IN 72!

A powerful collection of 12 slogans and 52 quotes. This pocket-size booklet contains statements that inspires and motivates the reader. Easy to carry and a great booklet to share with your associates.

BREAK 2 IN 72! (AUDIO CASSETTE VERSION)

A tape of inspiring quotes used as powerful affirmation statements. 52 quotes to strengthen you as you run your race in life. Use in your car during trips or when you want to relax and program positive encouraging thoughts into your mind. Uplifting!

YOU'VE GOT WHAT IT TAKES ...
TO MAKE A DIFFERENCE! (AUDIO CASSETTE)

This motivating and inspirational message challenges you to experience a life of meaning and purpose. Learn how you can know your presence in this world really matters. 30 minutes of encouragement from Steve Kime.

and coming soon! ....

FEEL GOOD ABOUT YOURSELF!

A booklet that contains powerful thoughts that may help change the way you feel about yourself. A must for anyone who has ever felt defeated and wanted a second chance in life! You can feel good about yourself ... again!

ABOUT STEVE KIME

Steve Kime, is an award winning radio broadcaster, a "record setting" athlete and Fortune 100 corporate trainer. Steve is known as an encourager and motivator. Today, he continues to encourage audiences with his motivational messages that "make the difference."

Steve was active in all sports and set individual and team track records. During his broadcasting career, Steve produced two radio commercials that were voted "Best Radio Commercials" in the state of Oklahoma and for which he was presented an award by the Oklahoma Broadcasters Association. He has served as a corporate trainer for a Fortune 100 company.

Steve shares his expertise, energy and enthusiastic messages in powerful seminars and keynotes all across the country. He has spoken to audiences throughout the United States, the Caribbean and Central America. Steve is a member of the American Society of Training and Development and the National Speakers Association. He is an author and columnist for a national newspaper.

For more information about Steve's training
or speaking please contact:

Steve Kime
P. O. Box 52552
Tulsa, OK 74152-0552
(918) 747-9076 • (800) 329-9235
e-mail: kimespeakr@aol.com

Keeping a Journal
• • •

"Learn as much by writing as by reading."
- Lord Acton

Several years ago I was challenged by a friend to begin writing down experiences in a journal that I encountered daily. They explained to be the numerous benefits of "journaling" which included documenting the personal growth I would be experiencing as the days pass by. By taking the time to record relationship experiences, emotions felt on a particular day, and lessons learned from significant events, I would begin to observe the changes my life was undergoing.

"Journaling" is an excellent way to record personal victories or even those bitter disappointments that pass our way. Documenting these experiences gives us an opportunity to note our responses to these events. Our reaction to many of life's events can either make us bitter or make us better. When you write down your responses to such moments, it becomes an avenue of learning and living.

From time to time, I look back through the daily journals I have kept for years. As I looked through the pages of my journal recently, I began reading about events in those days that passed long ago. I reminiscensed about the day I witnessed a magnificent eagle getting ready to soar all alone in the sky. It was just me and the eagle that cool, crisp morning. What a precious event in my life! I was able to relive that moment only because I took the time to write down that early morning experience.

And now here is an opportunity for you to begin your daily journal. This is an opportunity to document the exciting events about to take place in your life. Keeping a journal is like going on a journey. Get ready for a fascinating and exciting trip down the highway of life!

When Winston Churchill was Prime Minister of England, it was reported that he was confident that history would deal kindly to this leader. When asked why he believed that history would be good to him his reply was, "Because I intend to write it." Let me encourage today to begin writing. Write about your experiences and you too will be writing your history.

As always wishing you the very best!

Steve Kime

JOURNAL

JOURNAL

JOURNAL

JOURNAL

Journal

JOURNAL

JOURNAL

JOURNAL

— 94 —

JOURNAL

— 95 —

JOURNAL